When I
Smoked Pot
with My Daughter

Also by Shelley Townsend-Hudson

Books:

When I Got Drunk with My Mother:
      Poems About Growing Up Southern
Companions for the Soul (with Robert Hudson)

Chapbooks:

When I Got Drunk with My Mother
Into
From the Window
This Southern Thing About Shoes
Paths Before We Knew Them
Hibriten

When I Smoked Pot with My Daughter

Poems About Parenting

Shelley Townsend-Hudson

PERKIPERY PRESS / CHAPBOOK PRESS
2024

Chapbook Press

Schuler Books
2660 28th Street SE
Grand Rapids, MI 49512
(616) 942-7330
www.schulerbooks.com

When I Smoked Pot with My Daughter

Published in association with the Perkipery Press.

ISBN 13: 9781957169941
eBook ISBN: 9781957169958

Library of Congress Control Number: 2024920005

For inquiries, contact the author at:
        Perkipery Press
        8405 Baileau Oaks Dr. NE
        Ada, MI   49301
        hudsbob@comcast.net

Some of the poems appeared in these chapbooks: *Hibriten* (2004), *Paths before We Knew Them* (2005), *This Southern Thing about Shoes* (2006), *From the Window* (2007), *Into* (2008), and *When I Got Drunk with My Mother* (2010), all available from the Perkipery Press.

Cover design by Mark Sheeres

Printed in the United States of America.

To
Abigail Townsend Hudson
Molly Abernethy Hudson
and
Lili Huaying Hudson

Introduction ⟿

I don't remember many specific things my parents tried to teach me as I was growing up. All I remember is *who* they were. They just lived and let me watch them.

My own parenting approach has been much the same, though I like to think I was a bit more playful. When my children were small, I liked to get down on their level and be spontaneous, goofy, and creative.

As they grew older we had tough times for sure. I began keeping a journal in which I poured out my dark thoughts and frustrations, but later, I decided to keep a gratitude journal instead. I filled pages and pages of spiral-bound notebooks with lists of things I was thankful for – little things, like light and shadow playing on a wall, a bumblebee on a chicory flower, a dog curled at my feet, asking forgiveness from a daughter, on and on.

Sometimes I pull out these notebooks and read over the old lists that chronicle our lives. These glimpses jar my memory about where we were and what we were doing as a family. They are filled with light and joy. The bad moments – which I called "hard *eucharisteo*" (thankfulness) – are interspersed in the listings, training me to be grateful for the good and the bad. I hope my children remember the light more than the dark – though really, you can't see one without the other.

– Shelley Townsend-Hudson, October 2024

When I
Smoked Pot
with My Daughter

First Birth ~⤚

I was reshelving books when I felt you
in the *T* section of picture books,
a snowflake sifting down inside,
a quickening so biblical sounding

you were announcing yourself
as the third of two
who in relationship caused you to be
you were you, but we began to call you Um
Baby Um, not knowing
if you were him or her or them

Later a sonogram
and hearing your choo-choo heart
and we read to you
and daddy put his lips to you
to wish you goodnight

And summer-borne you came
thunder carrying a lightning branch
that pushed you here
our jolt
our brag
our joy

After the Birth ⟡

My sisters came when my first child
was born. How amazed they were that you
can't see across Lake Michigan. That night
we lay on the ground, watching shooting

stars, the sky as ripe as when I went into
labor. My newborn lay next to me
We cried out each time a star dropped, afraid
to look away or even blink for fear of missing one

I loved us there on the ground, hurtling
through space, even my heavy beloved
brother-in-law holding his place and
my infant, waving in the dark

Small Thoughts for Abbie

You've wanted all your good things
in one place. Like when you tried to suck
your thumb and nurse at the same time.
It certainly seemed possible.

Your hands were open, ready to receive
but obstacles came, and slowly you
learned that fluttering wings
shaped the will.

As surely as you pressed against me
betrayals were that near. Would that
a shawl, warm breath, the heartbeat
made all things possible.

Weighing In

An Amish woman rides the ferry
her full skirt billows
a child rests on her hip
I've got mine on mine
they weigh about the same

She'll go home to light her lantern
I will flick a switch
we'll both bathe our babies in light

I'd gladly trade my ways for hers
she would not for mine
I have burdens
but she has hers

they weigh about the same

First-Child Mistakes

Sometimes it helps to push the zipper all
the way down into the little case before you
pull it up – that was all you needed to hear
in your misery with your jacket. The more
we tried to push your feelings away the more
stuck you got. As you grew we let you figure out
for yourself what you needed or wanted.
Any direction yielded surprises. We lost track
of matching feeling for feeling. Rather we watched
you gliding forth with amazement.

At Breast (Molly)

(Luke 2:19)

What scene would I rather be enveloped by
than this one: my new baby nursing and she,
having caught my eye, grins. It was all there.
My heartbeat beneath her cheek, her
hand atop my breast. Other moments
come and come and come, offering
themselves to me, and I've stored them up.

Grace (Molly, age 3)

Who was I but a mother,
who'd gotten the rhythm down,
drifting through day-to-day.
Lamentable, at midlife, to still
be bent on missing the moment.

Come to the window, Molly
insisted. What is it? Just come!
Wearily, I gave in, and there
sat a red fox scratching its ear,
so near to that child and me
we could almost spy the flea.

Note for Molly ~_cc~

Your tiny piano key fell out today.
   It was still singing in the little envelope,
while you stood beaming in carpool line.

Later you cried. I, grieving too, wrote
"First Lost Tooth" on the envelope with a note:
You held eternity in the palm of your hand.

Alight (Abbie) ~~~

A butterfly landed on your shoulder
You were seven or eight. You knew
to barely breathe. No one talked or coughed
or sneezed, while I snapped the picture

What most resembles the butterfly?
It is wonder, as in dust motes,
a sun dog, the morning star
As in your face with its exquisite
tilt, motionless and so composed

Long Week in Kindergarten

Molly came home Monday
having given away her first kiss.
Tuesday presented a problem
with Philip and another girl.

Wednesday, Philip decided to marry Ruth,
but Molly, full of triumph, held his hand
in carpool line on Thursday.

Oh, but Friday. Not good. Philip said
he'd marry Molly but only after Ruth died.
And that could be 100 years.
At least.

Captive Audience ~≈

Molly recuperates in a hospital bed
(you never know where motherhood will land you),
a needle in her small fist, IV vine-climbing a pole.
Across the hall a nurse lifts a baby, pats her behind,
and rocks her in the waning light,

jarring this memory: My mother is dying in the hospital,
out her window, another window frames a scene;
a new mother divvies attention between
the small bundle on her bed and the TV on the wall.
Odd, what captivates the eye.

Lapsit ~~~

These passions sit in my lap
Love is bouncy, likes
Trot to Town and
This is the Way

Anger, a big-mouthed O,
beats my breast
hangs upside down
slides off

I can never get away
from Prayer
Ubicumque me verto ades –
Wherever I turn, there you are –
always here in my lap

Seeing Stars (Lili)

You never suspect how it
will hit you the first time
you see your newborn's face.

Somewhere in the clouds
in highest heaven they learn
to slay with a gaze.

You'd not expect to be knocked
flat by a two-by-four
inch mug shot of the child

you plan to adopt. But you
will be ensnared just as certain
as a halo encircles the moon.

One Swaying Being

On the Great Wall of China, the children forged
ahead with their daddy over the tilting slabs. Leaning
on my hands, I let the wind pour its wine.
An engraver nodded and displayed his etchings.

Focusing on the mountains I half-believed were
the Smokies, Chinese graffiti under my palms, the
beaming artist, and children shrinking down the
Wall, left me drunk and dizzy with abundance.

Bus Ride in China ⨪⨿

We rolled past rice fields
to our daughter's first home, past
storefronts along the barely-there
road. Women lifted their eyes like

tiny moons rising night after night.
One among them could be the mother
of our child, having followed shadows
and placed her small baby wrapped

in red by the orphanage gate.
A paper clip from dossiers joined
our lives forever. Once home,
our balance still uncertain in the tides

of sleepless nights, we finally
adjusted to our hemisphere. But the
pull between us remained always, she, in
her morning, and we, in our night.

Red Thread ⟿

The little girl is made in China
The dress is made in America
The girl is two and the dress, twenty,
joined together by common threads

How did this come about,
this ups-a-daisy over arms
down round shoulders, unveiling
a small upturned moon-face?

Ying-Ying in a hand-me-down
from a grown cousin, with delicate
embroidery on the pinafore, sewn by
a grandmother she'll never know

who tongue-moistened a red thread
guiding it into a needle, never dreaming
of a shiny-haired child, twirling
in a mirror, in a dress made in America

Who ties these invisible threads, ankle to
ankle, pinky to pinky? Deity Yue Lao
who, adopting us, pieces us together at a
certain time, in a particular way

with bonds that stretch, tangle, knot,
but never break, stitching mystery
to mercy, desire to destiny, the likely to
the unlikely. Handmade on this patched planet

Aisle 4 ～〜

 bbie and her friends in Jiffy Stop searched
 for bubblegum soda. I followed, toddler in arms,
admiring how their ponytails swayed with their out-of-school
bounce. They suddenly stopped, Three Stooges style.

"Oh, that's my mother's aisle," my grinning girl said.
The aisle of disdain, Tide, 409, All, Xtra, Gain lane.
I smiled back, her words not yet registering.
But I'd noticed the pink stain on her "Girls Rule" shirt.

Though a pace or two ahead, I knew she'd heard me:
"Hey, wait, that's not what my life's about."

In bed at night, remembering the slight, sweet roll
of her eyes, I sermonized myself: Life is but a carving
out of emptiness. Though inspired to sacrifice,
I'm no bodhisattva. I fall short of openheartedness,

searching aisle after aisle for a cure for imperfection.
My deep soul hangs on a line, having been soaked
and scrubbed and wrung time and again. It billows
on air next to the size 8 shirt with its proud slogan.

Mourning (for my adopted daughter)

You were on my lap, Ming vase,
so fragile with your dirty ankles,
and the hotel hall was filled
with crying orphans placed in
arms of strangers who had odd smells,

foreign tongues, and blanched hair.
Everything was changed. You became
a dream where a detail was missing,
if we could only conjure it, we
could unlock your past.

Though we went home, China
would be like wind playing spy,
opening and closing doors.
Like the mourning dove whose
song retrieves distance across the roof,

what you wanted to understand
was a window that would never receive
the sun. I could not open blinds or
push back curtains to lighten the panes.
The house noises that were once

love songs for me had stopped.
As soon as my foot touched the floor
the walls awoke and the dream
became hollow on the outside.
All around life reconvened.

Wherever you went, molecules
of you whirled in ecstasy, boundaries
no longer begrudged you, and faces,
friendly, curious, intrusive, beguiled you
into believing you did not need

to be the daughter of anyone.
Your charm was a kind of truth,
yet physical appearance is a cloud
before the soul's eye. Like Van Gogh's
cypresses where sadness hides,

you would find me waiting like
a small fire in the clearing. Never
the true mother like your secret one,
but one from whom you'd receive
transfusions. Anger broke attunement,

but reconnection brought new life,
and through the other we became
what we were born for. On the Great
Wall of China uneven stones forced
me to drop to all-fours. Graffiti,

scratched in stone, I could not decipher,
Mongolia undulated along
the horizon: I never knew how lost
I was, how risky the path, how vertigo
insisted, Be alive. We are still

with you in the holding room.
All five of us make a stronger circle
to be lost in. Something more than
had been known before, comforts us.
And we will not let you go.

Abbie at Ten

This is the year you were up and down
pogo-sticking eighty-six times on the drive.
What is it your energy seeks?

This is the year you loved Ying-Ying, your
Chinese sister you comforted and protected,
took in hand, brushed hair from eyes.

Your best friend was Jaspreet, girl from India,
the two of you, ambitious, full of questions.
What is it your wonder seeks?

This is the year you loved Greek myths,
with your thoughts you created new worlds,
thick, rich, gathering midsummer light.

You played Puck, danced in church, ice skated,
picked a perfect kitten, mastered skip-counting.
Whatever you seek while standing, walking,

cherish good-will and lovingkindness.
In your spinning, twirling days each hour
is a pearl from the South China Seas.

On the Swing (Molly) ⌇

Your shadow went out from your body,
   Molly, in front and behind, as the swing
lifted you from the ground. "I hate thunder,"

you said. "God shouldn't have made it.
When I grow up, I'm going to be a nun
who doesn't believe in God." The shaft

     of your sweet anger revealed
     the holiness of your opinion
     keeping your secret life alive.

Later, under bedcovers, grieving
at turning six, never again to be five,
you held your passion in a breathless

space while Daddy comforted you,
singing, "Never grow old, never grow old,
in a land where we'll never grow old."

And later still, as the sun and thin moon were
shut off by black clouds, you wrote, "The sun
and moon are high but God is still higher."

Your shadow went out from your body,
Molly, in front and behind, lifting and
lifting again your feet from solid ground.

Parting after Adoption Reunion 〜

(August 2003)

We came together in the summer
an extended family formed by the thread
we'd all followed the year before
our children having grown taller with longer dark
hair since a whole half of the universe
had swept the sun and passed again

We'd discussed potty training, sleeping
problems, their hearty appetites and zeal,
never following out the strangeness
stirring in our deepest brains. What I meant
was, this space shuttle we were all on,
maiden voyage and the world going by

As we dispersed one pig-tailed girl
with a zig-zaggy part stood twirling
among the others who'd all lived in an
orphanage. This came to mind:
the Great Wall as seen from space,
stitches across the face of the earth

Rising Moon

(September 11, 2003)

We celebrated Ying-Ying's first Moon Festival
with Boston Crème pie frosted with a full
yellow moon and traditional mooncakes too.

After the pie, traces of moon glazing her lips, she
desired mooncake. "Yuck!" Not so sweet.
We laughed at her bright round face.

Toys on the Floor

I hate plastic polymerized toys
(except Mr. Potato Head with his bright plastic senses).
The beepers, squawkers, computer-chip tutors,
and navigators of their own accord, all annoy.

Give me a wood toy made by an elf,
hunched over his lathe in a snow-laden hut,
who understands the joy of turning and exploding grain.
Little maple burl curls lay at his up-turned feet.

His masterpieces are scattered on our floor –
blocks, cobbler bench, shape sorters, stackers.
I'd rather trip on them than high-density polyethylene
that neither feeds the eye nor magnifies the soul.

Listening Eyes ⚮

(Shaker Village, 2004)

W here is quiet with this cricket
in the room, cockroach
in the sheets, and restless children
waiting to eat?

It is there in the Shaker
slat-back chair where an angel sits,
halo looped on a peg, under
a circle of light on the ceiling.

Repose ~~✑

*B*onnet on a Shaker peg,
    still life, deeply rooted,
hanging for all angles of a tourist's lens,
but while no one's looking, I tie it
on our child, and my camera
swallows up, full-aperture,
her deep black eyes, beauty
beyond the shutter's release
to the power of standing
still, true inseeing.

Dear Eleven-Year-Old (Abbie)

You won't read this for another
eleven years, or more, or never
but what you wrote on scrap paper –
your wish to be a missionary someday –
made me smile

But I had to laugh at what followed
such lofty ambition,
Olympic skater, fashion model –
what you do is you, for that you came –
may it always transport you to wonder

Make-Up (Abbie)

We couldn't see her face
as she moved in the morning,
packing lunch, collecting
books, her back turned,
head down in a veil of hair.

A younger sister plunked
a plastic piano, another
waited for a bagel, leaning
in to watch her nose
in the toaster's flank.

She hoped we wouldn't notice,
say eleven was too young,
say sun was blush enough,
yet we did, and though
the rose deepened in

her cheeks her eyes revealed
relief in being kept from
a thing too soon. Her body's
ripe listening turned back
to us like morning glory.

With Molly at the Playground
(Spring 2005)

You told me you liked the jungle gym,
    how good the pole felt between your legs.
You told me it made you laugh just to climb.
Someday I'll explain how all your balloons
will let loose. But not now. Yellow, red,
and blue, I clutched the strings you let me
hold and listen to their joyful bobbling.

The Challenge

If I can love this sick child
  at 1:00 a.m.
then I can love my own ill-natured side.

1-2-3 Rocks

I bought four rocks
engraved with words.
One with Peace, one, Gratitude,
one read Think, another, Share.
Paid good money for them,

with an idea in mind: a child can
meditate, rock in sweaty palm,
swinging her leg in the time-out chair.
You can't draw blood from a rock,
but you can wish for magic.

From the Window ⌒⌐

They weren't bickering for
a change, playing hopscotch
in the drive, dropping bottle caps,
and pirouetting on the final block.

Their lips moved but made no
sound, as if in a dustglobe,
sand spewing from their heels.
      And God gently lifted her ball,

shook it, sending caps and hopscotch
lines spiraling, each child parachuting
into her own perfect narrative,
drifting easily, free of the weight

of the face in the window, lower
and lowering until they rested
on their own star, harnessed
and swaying in the sparkling light.

Lili

*B*rown puddle
   red boots
splash

Asian Flag

Dressed in red
  pockets
full
of
bright
yellow
stars
she waves
from
the schoolyard

Soul of a Child (Molly)

*C*hildren who are not so sensitive
have a way in the world. Complex
in their own right, they reflect well
upon others. Their parents are more
than willing to accept the credit.

But a complicated child can't always
fathom herself, running so deep.
At age seven she might say she hates
herself when she should still be
believing she's just about perfect.

You feel how steep the hills will be
for her and ache, knowing a whole
range lies ahead. Like a small bird
alone on the roof, you see the line
of clouds in the distance.

It's in the spider song, thumb meeting
finger in a tiny benediction. Forget
about the falling, the sun's still
sovereign. Trust. This child, who feels
the spaces, in due time, will climb.

Watching Molly ～⌒

(March 12, 2006)

You believed in fairies,
   placing enticements
in the yard. Girl after our heart

The next day you could not
find the note you'd left for them;
it was blown by the wind

(into our safekeeping)
As you searched for it
we ached, seeing you fish

through your little
pile of pebbles while
peepers throstled

We had to look away
when your face tilted
toward the treetops

The trembling under
oak leaves and light
playing off them

was useless to capture
any more than to capture
sun in your hair

Half-awake, half-asleep
was your life – here, always
here and watched over

Another Move Won't Do It ~✑

That old Gothic farmhouse is now for sale
the one I drive by so often, point out
to the children, it's a gingerbread house.
The realtor called the trim "lacy vergeboard" as
I was led inside to feel the breathing space

and looked up at peaked sun blocks on the walls.
Back home, folding laundry, I moved in,
painted the bedrooms, imagined the children
clamoring down the stairs, hands on the worn
newel as they arced toward the kitchen.

But my own house, silent now, with its morning light
feeds me like a revelation, the children swing
against a backdrop of trees, our five dogwoods
quietly drop their petals
I savor the place I am.

You Have to Be Careful ✑

I am not a stage mom but wait
in the wings because I want my child
to have what her heart yearns for.
But how does a floodlight tell anyone
how to live a life?

Some model parents say,
if our children have confidence
they can do anything. Our role
is to excavate their talents.

So. This has something to do
with the journey to the self?
A gathering of props? costumes,
wigs, make-up? There are many ways
of becoming adults, true, but

parents, in your career of worrying,
or comparing or competing
any lack in your child might grow
teeth. Remember they still feel
the softest air.

The dreamer, noticer of things,
who's not always sure of the way
but honors another's way,
her humility may never trump
achievement, but neither does it
come up full of empty.

Father of Flower Girls (for Bob)

They came as you'd expect:
the eldest, poised, self-contained;
the second, bashful, sweet;
the youngest, ripping down full-throttle.

Basho said, For the man
who says he tires
of his children there are no flowers.

Afterward you bent for a petal
or two from roses that once reached
deep for their color and slipped
them in your pocket.

At Wheatland (for Abbie)

(September 2006)

Mommy, dance?"
   Always and of course.
Would that you could
always be thirteen,
wanting to flatfoot.

Tell your children, your
grandchildren, how we danced
to old-time music
at the festival.

The light along the hill
comes down slowly.
Someday you'll be grown.
Be content in a life
well-lived and recall
back then when our
black shoes
went flying.

In a Day

Seven and a half hours of errands in the car –
I could be halfway to Carolina from Michigan –
the time it took to complete my route with piano books
on the floorboard and a wet suit wrapped in a towel, the dog

as accompaniment, panting and bringing cheer
whenever the children clambered aboard and off.
There was a man on Fulton, early in the morning,
crossing the street. He had cerebral palsy, barely

making the light, so difficult a task it forbade me
to complain as I continued in my peripatetic way from
drop box to mail slot and down the road again to school.
On Leonard I saw him again, same blue shirt,

same pants, same dangling near-useless legs.
Strange how a burden you carry takes on hues.
You wonder about the world – how rare to receive
second reminders and how imperative to heed them.

Christmas Eve 2006 ⎯⎯⎯⎯

S he was more-than-ninety-four
   when she shared our meal.
Our three young children fixed
upon her until she began
slowly to regurgitate
then they swiftly exited.

We handed her napkin after napkin.
Each used one she placed
in the empty chair beside her,
continuing her storytelling.
Our dog snagged each one to carry
to his lair behind the couch.

I'd prayed for some small way
to make our advent more than a mere
wait for gifts. Our prayer returned
as second-hand manna, a funny story –
to tell and retell. What were we waiting for
after all, but love's dizzying shock?

Five-Part

While hail popcorned off the deck
we five watched, pleased with
white sight and sound

Abbie

(March 26, 2007)

You lost your last baby tooth,
what a sentimentalist, your mother,
to mark this event.

You'll laugh, but you don't know your own
majesty (I too forget mine). Your tooth
was a nugget unloosed from the crown.

While tulips, deep-red, were opening to
extremity so too were your beautiful lips,
revealing now their off-centered gap

Speech Therapy ⟿

(2007)

Molly no longer says,
"I'm 'tuck 'taring" when
her dreamy eyes rest upon
an object and she drifts
into sweet reverie

She outgrew the phrase
sometime around her sixth
birthday, unnoticed, like
blue velvet wind guttering
out candles

But one day after rain we beheld
a rainbow over the pond
our lambent wonder
kept us all 'tuck 'taring.

Mother's Prayer (Lili)

(Spring 2007)

In the ordinary course of things
    you forget what really matters.
But pushing you on the swing now
I wish that not one thing I've said
or done would be remembered
against me. But as I know it will, may
some better moment come back as well,
like when you stood singing in the yard,
convinced the robin, whose nest
you were too near, was singing back to you,
how you ran to tell me. May you trust
bonuses, like sunrises, which bear
up to many losses and expand our lives

Napping

The dog next door barked,
  a yellow jacket bumped the screen,
the cat lent her presence on the sheet.
Quiet, like pooled breath on the edge

of the quilt, came in. As if on cue,
a nuthatch landed on the sill.
We stared an instant, cat and I, before it
flew. Had it spoken, it might have said –
be one on whom no thing is lost.

Molly ⟋⟋⟋

Molly, make your decisions.
Say no to what you don't want.
You don't project
a strong exterior, but you've
strength in your quietness.
A still deep pool
lying flat, spreading
thin but deep

Birthday Celebration (Abbie)

(June 14, 2007)

My sister and my daughter,
    sharing a birthday at the Hard
Rock Café – one had seen fifty
more years than the other but still
they both looked vulnerable
on the platform before this crowd

of revelers, mostly people we didn't
even know. Candles were flickering,
that was the picture, holding
its breath as we looked on. Later
finding the image on the back
of my camera, I felt every turn of

the earth that would come,
sensing something further inside
I could not define or explain, but
only let have its way, a helplessness,
a longing, a prayer: That the path
before them would not be risky.

Though they'd change without
my permission may they remain
connected and distinct.
May diminishments that come
make them fuller, like the summer
when life rose in us like tides

Sisters ～✦

(2007)

Summer and sisters, ten
  and fourteen, embraced each day
like passing pearls between you.
Now you wear a string of them
on the inside, lustrous, love leaking
out unguarded,
it won't ever be the same summer again

of giggling behind closed doors and glances,
measuring us in different ways now
where trips to the beach, the park, or
the woods was more about you
than us, which was why we had you
both in the first place. We will leave

summers to come back to this one,
taking you into ourselves as you were,
sunlit like grapes. Who made
these changes? we'll wonder, tasting
each sweet orb, and how does a better
self keep getting better?

En Route with Molly ⤳

We were quiet in the car
I watched you in the mirror
with your small face upturned
your eyes following clouds

to where there was no connection
down to leafless trees, each
second filled with the last
in the slow eye of youth

In my childhood there were no
seat belts, only a beefy rope
slung the length of the seat
to cling to in the curves

but you, secured, race along
this hurry-through with rare
and common things passing
too fast to fix in the mind

I've tried to keep the way steady
but as you ride on, remember
should fear ensnare, I hold you
forever in this reflection

Gestures

We gave our neighbor a smiley-face
balloon on which we'd written: Good
Luck Conquering Kilimanjaro.

Every day, passing his house, we
imagined where he might be in his climb,
each child in the car with her own

musings about a mountain in Africa.
On the day he came home he waved
from his drive, shouting how he'd thought

of us at the summit. We wondered,
had we been asleep? Having the dream
about the empty house with the piano or

about the dog flying out of the fire?
His thoughts on the summit and our dreams
had risen far to the stars, beyond

the Southern Cross, to a place where
the whole of our lives always returns
to whatever summit we've made.

The Sneeze (Prose Poem for Molly)

(2007)

Molly in a mood landmine too up and down hidden unbidden passion downwhirling upswirling tornado in glass jars moods here there yours mine on wings of dove or under a pile of envy loss aloneness depression joy sappers ingratitude deep deeper down up attuned see many things unnoticed by others and others don't really care you sweet noticer of things of light smells a sound like something else empty behind and around it isolated like how we heard a sneeze so loud on the empty street where on a Sunday morning the construction was still and I heard it and you commented on it weeks later the alone-sneeze that came from nowhere an isolated mood that you don't know arrived until you kicked it like a soccer ball or embraced it this thing you and you alone noticed but no one else cares for you will learn Molly no matter how much interest I take in what you hear see think taste the sneeze to other people does not amount to

but never stop doing it

In Dreamtime (Molly) ⟿

(2008)

I combed your just-washed hair as you played
piano, remembering the time I wandered
in a neighborhood more than twenty years
ago, pondering whether to marry your father
or not. Decisions never came readily to me

but that evening, as if in trance, I'd heard piano
spilling from a window, a child playing,
or so I imagined. Assurance came like a little
shell somewhere on the ocean floor opening
to take me in. Doing what we're meant

to do is a tiny drop of work in an ocean of tasks
we can't do, but a drop is significant enough.
When we're worn by the tinkering of a thing,
like the untangling of a stubborn snarl,
the shell opens and closes in currents.

And there you were with your fingers knowing
where to go on the keys, how miraculous to be
at your back, like sitting on the beach, my lap
filling with pearls and shells, saying, yes
to this, formed from a mere drop of myself.

Moon in the Water (Abbie at fifteen)

You are there at the mirror with
   that intrepid-looking lash curler,
remote, distant, not to mention
heavy scented
How could we think this time wouldn't come?
Individuating. Requiring us to mind it,
without minding it, impossible,
when what we want is you at the foot

of our bed again, laughing with your sister,
not behind a closed door, texting
how much you dislike us
In the midst of it, we repeat the mantra:
It's not about us, not about us
Light splays out in ten directions yet
how hard to see past this reflection

Right Words for a Daughter

Reading a book called
How Can You Say *That?*
a mother sought to put
right words in the balloon
above her head

Subtext always leaked
through the taut
surface, glum advocacy
seemed so pressing – why she
bought the book

in the first place. Words,
even with their pricking
edges, still held hope
that stumbling ways
could lead one home

It's there in chapter one:
how to state an apology,
arching over
the mother's head even as
the sun goes down.

At the Traffic Light
by the Middle School (Abbie) ⤳

In the next car – a woman on a phone.
   A teenage daughter text-messaged
from the passenger seat. All those words,
spoken, tapped, drifting over ponds and rooftops
and Canada geese, passage under passage.

We all turn pages we can't rewrite:
how I once gathered my child's hair
into a tiny sprout, or the O of her mouth
as the long-handled spoon flew in.
Yesterday she asked me how to shave her legs.

Our cars pulled away from the light. In the mirror,
the street, divided by a center line, traced
our directions. I'm either a tourist
or a pilgrim here, depending on the words
drifting out and away, passage under passage.

Attachment Disorder (Lili) ～

The way it is is this:
You're charming,
never met a stranger,
beloved by all. You want
to engage, but on your
terms.

The way it is is this:
You could just as well
go home with friendly
strangers than to be close
to the edge we share,
dull and sharp.

The way it is is this:
You make me turn
inside. I no longer look
and see you. It is always
me, looking, seeing myself
seeing you.

The way it is is this:
we are the stone awaiting
the chisel, chipping prayer
by prayer, by prayer
by another.

Pardon Us If We Ignore You

In the restaurant a woman leans in, Gucci
bag on lap, eyebrows lifted. We shift
our gaze and bodies away in anticipation
of: "Your daughter is so beautiful."

We've learned how it begins, how readily
some dismiss the obvious – that our family
consists of three girls, not just one exotic
Asian. We weary of this singling out,

as if, by a kind of winking they displace
some discomfort of their own.
"How admirable," these glances say,
which leaves us aching, nonetheless,

for the adopted child's voids we cannot fill,
for her always turning over stones
in wrong places.

No, Then Yes (Lili)

(Fall 2014)

W e hold hands you lean into me
sweet upturned face, my girl
you've something on your mind,
I read you like you read me

you say, no, but hold steady
you've always kept
your own wise counsel
and finally you say, yes
spreading gentleness around

Tongue-tied you confide you like
a boy – it's the first – to your middle-aged
mother, who is touched
that in this share of time

you've made me young again
waking from my sleep
heart-distractingly happy
you are happy. This no, then yes,
a gift, I will guard
holding your world in my arms

Offshore

Bobbing in the ocean at night
my husband and our three girls
the house alight on the shore

A solace, this living water, all salty
and warm, even with the blackness
and the knot in my floating heart

From the house my first family sent
someone to call us inside;
it's dangerous "out there"

A houseful of grinding, sweeping
secrets, backtalk, denials, waves
and breakers of unspoken hurts

The fear of riptides, not here, only
there, the undertow I'd finally
learned to ride out by swimming

sideways. But now my own
family here, weightless, rising swell
by swell, lifted and laughing

our foundation surely just as full
of cracks but all around an ocean
to call our own and no one to call us back

We Are Always Close to the Ground

The dog at the table on the chair
made us laugh with his sad eyes
The five of us silent, alone
but for the dog, who made us
lose our separateness

His chin on the maple top
eyebrows shifting
this way, that
our delight precisely
the joy the separate self
wanted to claim with others

Possible only because it flowed,
beginning with whatever
changed the condition
we became a part of: the wag,
the vibrancy, the riveted
nailed-down
now

Our Quaker Children ⁓⤳

These three fourth-dimensionalists,
in a three-dimensional world,
followers of proclivity, who adorn
Christ's head with their
asceticism of cheerfulness,

may they resist dull drumming
of melancholy, be single-minded
and watchful in a world
of inverted values, ready to bathe
his unattended feet in sunlight.

Last Things ⚯

This, our first child's last year home
leaves drop against a background of orange
where will she be when leaves change next fall?
A breeze brushes the earth's revolutions
we can't stop it picking up

if you don't look back, the future never happens
Was I grateful enough for this child?
Did she know it?

I was eleven when my father and I saw
a flying squirrel. Rare to see since they're nocturnal
They glide, not fly, and we watched it come
in for a landing on a tree trunk

The whole sky was hers
to glide into, blown open

Zen Parent

In the woods an occasional tree turns
    downward – crippled
among oaks – aiming for a sun patch
on the forest floor and learns

too late it's lost its way, awkward member
of the forest. Confusion made it curve
like a swan's neck and with each ring
it seeks lost timbre.

Willows don't bend for their own sake
despite a strong southern wind,
likewise, children act wisely without
worry and grow profusely by a lake.

Go bathe, admire your daughters and sons
singing in the emerald grove,
immerse your hands in the water
and break apart the sun's false suns.

Time-Out for Parents

*G*ive me the box of time
in which to place the ways we wish
we'd been better parents,
less critical and anxious

But first empty failures,
the times we bit air with
snappish opinions or
hurled heaps of shame

Once, after losing tempers,
we huddled in prayer,
it was awkward and only
a bandage, but the best

we could do. Years ago,
in our log house, we read
and sang to them, no other
place was better than there

They were small. A gaze
or a glance sent minor
messages back and forth,
automatic, full of affirmation

Now we strain sometimes,
feeling stuck, trying for amends
so beautiful and confusing
we need a new way

What if we let them think how
they like? We don't have
to match. It's only a bandage
but the best we can do

Being a Parent

Looking over your own shoulder,
  you measure and weigh, saying,
I could have done that better.
How exciting when you first set out
but it grows harder when the blazing sun
is about to set deeply, leaving
only a tenth of its light,
which makes some of the world far away
and the near only a hint. It helps to stop
thinking about there when you are here
and think of now instead of then
and to look again at yourself,
your one lamp turned low,
trying so hard at the trying.

Well: A Deep Subject

If I were a dowser my rod would turn
to three small children in the sand
and whenever I thirsted for visions
the windlass would draw them to me

When I Smoked Pot with My Daughter

Early fall on the back deck.
The sun low over the pond. I had not slept
for many nights. My grad-school daughter makes
an apple bong. I wondered, am I a horrible mother.
But no. It is oddly bonding. She, a grown woman
and me, vulnerable enough to ask for relief.

She chats about the bowl and neck,
the base and carb. In my day we just
rolled doobies. A fly bumps and buzzes
between the nearby screen and panes,
in the sky, orangish clouds, the last few
swallows zigzagging over the pond.
Her hands that once caressed my breast
nursing, carve expertly. My infant smiling
her toothless grin from the baby carrier
is now directing our own stoner film.
I feel the sun between my shoulder blades.
What scene would I rather be enveloped by than this,
you carrying me as I carried you.

Remembering Our Babies (to Bob)

The first would not open her eyes for days,
now nothing misses her scrutiny.

The second would babble only at night
with the silent house to herself.

The third, small Asian, woke our neighborhood
with the sound of clapping.

In the depths of ourselves we have entered
three doors, this secret house of bliss.

Lili, Abbie, Molly ⌒

Acknowledgments ⤳

Parenting, I believe, is all about how close our worse selves are to our better selves. There is always that tension. So I'm grateful to my coparent, Bob Hudson, who restores that balance for me with his thoughtful guiding hand. As I do for him. And no, marijuana did *not* come into play as we navigated the many challenges of parenting!

I am grateful to Dr. Don Riggs of Drexel University, poet, professor, and master of the sonnet, who writes daily Facebook poems that are so phenomenal, witty, and thought-provoking that they catch me off-guard every day. Whether he knows it or not, he challenges me with his discipline to *get writing*.

I also want to thank Dr. Paul Willis, poet and emeritus professor of English at Westmont College, for finding delight in my poem "Long Week in Kindergarten" and then being willing to read more of my poems on childrearing. As a grandparent, he remembers the challenges and frustrations of parenting and now reaps the joy of grandparenting. Crossing that finish line, whether grandchildren come or not, is where we find our very best selves.

The cover artwork is by the amazing Mark Sheeres, who also illustrated three of Bob's books. Thank you so much, Mark.

And finally, to publishing wiz Pierre Camy, who has shepherded both of my books through the production process, I send a big thank you.

About Shelley Townsend-Hudson ～⇜

Shelley Townsend-Hudson was born in Lenoir, North Carolina. Her father, a small-town attorney, a gentleman farmer, and a lover of poetry, named her in honor of Percy Bysshe Shelley. Her father was a friend of Thomas Wolfe's at the University of North Carolina in 1919.

Shelley's childhood home was on a road called Tremont Circle, which wound around a hill at the foot of Hibriten Mountain, just east of Lenoir.

Today she is a musician, a dancer, and an award-winning poet. Her poems have appeared in various literary journals and in a series of chapbooks published by the Perkipery Press. Her previous book of poetry is called *When I Got Drunk with My Mother.*

Shelley sings and plays banjo in the old-time string band Gooder'n Grits, which performs for dances and festivals throughout West Michigan.

She enjoys showing her Welsh Terriers in AKC and UKC conformation classes, barn hunt, Fast CAT, and tracking events.

She is married to author Robert Hudson, and they have three daughters, Abbie, Molly, and Lili. Shelley and Robert split their time between Ada, Michigan, and Old Salem, North Carolina., depending on the weather.

www.ingramcontent.com/pod-product-compliance
Lightning Source LLC
Chambersburg PA
CBHW051008140626
46546CB00016B/1297